CONTENTS

How to look at trees

The trees we see all around us are large plants in which the hard, woody stalk (the trunk) divides first into branches, then into twigs which bear the leaves.

Whole tree		– Is the **crown** pointed, rounded, or spread out? – Are the **branches** upright, hanging or twisted? – Does the **trunk** divide? What is the **bark** like? (colour, texture . . .)
Leaves		– Are they **simple** (a) or **compound** (b)? – Are they **alternate** (c) or **opposite** (d)? – How large are they? – Are they **deciduous** or **evergreen**? (Do they fall in the winter or not?)
Flowers		–When do they appear? (This may vary from one part of the country to the other.) – How are they formed? (Note particularly flowers which will change into fruits.)
Fruits/Seeds		– When do the fruits ripen? What shape are they? What colour? Are they hard or soft? – How many seeds are there inside the fruit? What shape are they? What colour? How do they germinate?
Location		– In its natural state, does the tree grow in a dry or damp, open or shady position? – How was it planted? Where did it come from? – Do any animals use it for shelter? Or for food? – Has it any diseases (galls, fungi . . .)?
Uses		– Is it an ornamental tree? – Do we use the bark, the leaves, the flowers, the fruits? What do we use them for? – Is the wood used as a raw material? What sort of things are made from it?

Gather some twigs and leaves and make a herbarium. Collect some dry fruits and seeds. See if they will germinate.

The Common Oak

If you want to get to know a tree, you must look at it carefully throughout the year. If you stand at a distance, you will see the whole tree. Then, as you get nearer, you will see the different parts, one by one.

The Common Oak (a) is a very large tree, anything up to 40m (130 ft) tall. It likes plenty of light. It can live for a very long time (500 to 1,000 years). The wood is hard and strong, and used in building and furniture-making.

The **crown** consists of **large, twisting branches.** The foliage grows in clusters. The **bark** is smooth at first, but soon becomes deeply fissured.

The **leaves** are alternate (see page 3) and have a short stalk and a deeply lobed blade. They turn a dull brown in autumn and are slow to fall. In winter, the Common Oak can easily be identified by the pointed, many scaled **buds** clustered at the tips of the twigs. (b, c)

a. The oak in Spring

b. A bud opening

c. Young leaves

d. Male flowers

e. Female flowers (x 5): they will gradually change into fruits. You can see the remains of the flower on the acorn

The **flowers** appear in late April or early May. The long, hanging, yellow-green **catkins** (d) produce pollen which is carried by the wind. These are the male flowers. The small, round, scaly female flowers (e), from which short spikes develop, grow on the same twig.

In the autumn the acorns ripen and fall from their cups. Acorns are **fruits** containing a **seed**. There was a time when people used them to feed pigs. In the wild, they are eaten by wild boars, by birds (such as jays), and by many kinds of insect larvae.

f. Acorns in summer

g. Ripe acorns in the autumn

1. Draw a picture or a diagram to show how an acorn grows.

The walnut

leaflets making up the compound leaf

Appearance	– The walnut is a very beautiful tree, which often reaches a height of 20 to 30 m (100 ft). – The crown is broad and rounded. – The bark is smooth and light in colour.
Leaves	– The large, deciduous leaves are alternate and composed of 5 to 9 light green leaflets. They are very tough, and have a pleasant smell.
Flowers	– Appear in late April, early May. – Develop at the same time as the leaves. – Female flowers: 1 to 4 flowers at the tip of the twig. – Male flowers: long, hanging catkins with several stamens. The pollen is carried by the wind.
Fruits/Seeds	– A soft, green, fleshy fruit ripens in October. – Its thick wall, or husk, is sweet-smelling and its juice stains the fingers. This fruit turns black and decays, revealing the kernel or nut. – The kernel contains the seed, which is made up of two cotyledons, rich in oil. The nuts are a favourite food of crows and small rodents.
Location	– It likes light. – It has been cultivated in Europe since Roman times, and probably came from Asia. – It can live for two hundred years.
Uses	– We eat the nut, and extract the oil. – The wood is very hard and is used in furniture-making.

female flowers, each with two long feathery tufts

a male catkin

a twig in Springtime

the young shoot begins to grow

the shell splits

the nut germinates easily

the main root grows deep down into the soil

2. What part of the plant are you eating when you eat a nut?

a. A twig in winter

b. Leaves

c. Male flowers

d. Female flowers

e. Young fruits. Note the remains of
the flower at the top of each nut

f. Fruit cut in half to show seed

The Sweet Chestnut

This tree can reach a height of 25 to 30m (100 ft), and live for several hundred years. In old trees the trunk is huge. The Sweet Chestnut will live in any **non-chalky soil**. Where it grows **on its own,** the **crown** of the tree is very broad, with big branches spreading upwards. In **woodlands**, it is often grown as coppice; then its rapid growth makes it very suitable for fencing, parquet floors, packaging etc.

On old trees, the **bark** is dark brown with deep vertical fissures. The young twigs are reddish in colour.

The **leaves** are deciduous (see page 3) and arranged alternately on the stem. They are long—sometimes as much as 25cm (10 in) and pointed, with a sharp serrated edge.

It **flowers** in June or July (a). The same twig will bear both
- **male flowers**, tall, upright **catkins**, with many sweet-smelling stamens, and
- **female flowers,** which grow in groups of three at the base of the catkins. They are enclosed within a small, green, scaly sheath, with lighter-coloured filaments growing in between.

The chestnuts, which ripen in October, are enclosed within the sheath of the female flower, which has now become a hard, spiny husk. These are the **fruits.** We eat their **seeds**.

a. A chestnut in flower. Note the many stamens on the catkins, and the small, greenish, female flowers

3. Compare the Sweet Chestnut and the Horse Chestnut (see page 24).

b. Young twigs in Springtime

d. Young fruit and a withered male catkin

e. Ripe chestnuts, each with six little spikes on top

c. Upright male catkins (x 2)

9

The White Willow

The White Willow is very common on river banks and in other damp places. It is quite a small tree—10 to 20m (30 to 60 ft) tall, and has silvery grey bark.

The leaves are deciduous, simple and alternate (see page 3). They are long and pointed and hairy underneath. The buds are reddish in colour, and lie close to the twig (a).

The flowers appear in March or April, male and female on separate trees. The **male catkins** are yellow (b) and the **female catkins** are green and silky, with small bottle-shaped pistils. Insects carry the pollen from the male to the female flowers. These will develop into seed-boxes, which will open to release hundreds of fluffy little seeds. The seeds are capable of germinating immediately.

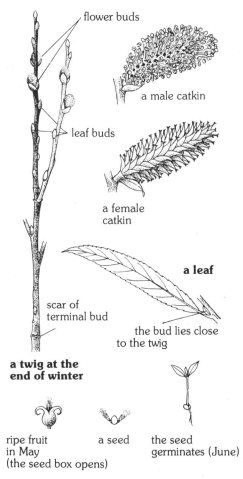

flower buds

a male catkin

leaf buds

a female catkin

a leaf

scar of terminal bud

the bud lies close to the twig

a twig at the end of winter

ripe fruit in May (the seed box opens)

a seed

the seed germinates (June)

a

b

4. Compare the way pollen is carried in the willow and the oak (see page 5).

The aspen

The aspen is a graceful tree about 20 to 30m (60 to 100 ft) tall. The **branches** are slender and few in number. The **bark** is smooth and light in young trees, but later becomes dark grey and fissured.

The aspen likes light and humidity. It grows quickly and the wood is very suitable for making paper pulp. It is often grown especially for this purpose.

The **leaves**, which vary in size and shape, are simple and alternate. The long, flattened leaf-stalks cause the leaves to flutter in the slightest breeze.

The **flowers** are long, **hanging catkins** which appear in March and April before the leaves. The male and female flowers grow on different trees. The male catkins are brown, and the female catkins are green.

The **fruits**, which ripen in May, take the form of seed-boxes containing very many little black **seeds**. The seeds are fluffy and carried by the wind.

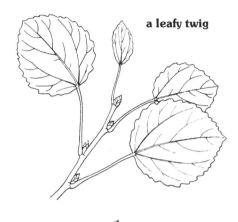

a leafy twig

a male catkin with red stamens

a. Young leaves

b. Female catkins bearing fruit

CONIFER
The Scots Pine

The Scots Pine is one of the most commonly grown conifers, as it will adapt itself to any type of soil. It likes **plenty of light**, however, and hates competition from other trees. In hilly areas, it is more likely to be found on sunny slopes. It produces **high quality wood**, and large quantities are used in the building industry.

The Scots Pine is easily recognized by its tall, slender shape, its reddish bark which is thick and flaky, and by its blue-green needles.

The leaves, or needles, are arranged in pairs. They are sharp and slightly twisted, measuring 3 to 8 cm (2 to 3 in) in length.

The flowers appear in the Spring.

– The male flowers are yellow, and produce a large amount of fine, dust-like pollen, which is carried by the wind.

– The female flowers, which are round and red, are found at the tips of the young shoots. It takes two and a half years for the cone or fruit to mature. The cones hang down, and are made up of scales, each containing two winged seeds. These are released when the cone opens. They germinate at some distance from the parent tree – unless they have been eaten beforehand by squirrels and fieldmice, or birds such as woodpeckers and crossbills.

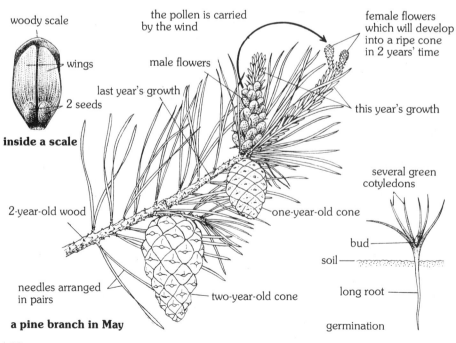

woody scale

the pollen is carried by the wind

female flowers which will develop into a ripe cone in 2 years' time

wings

male flowers

last year's growth

2 seeds

inside a scale

this year's growth

several green cotyledons

2-year-old wood

one-year-old cone

bud

soil

needles arranged in pairs

two-year-old cone

long root

a pine branch in May

germination

12

a. Male flowers in Spring

b. Female flowers

c. Male flowers (x 2)

d. Female flowers (x 1.5)

e. One-year-old fruit

f. Two-year-old fruit, releasing its winged seeds

5. Would it be possible to find a Scots Pine, a Common Oak (page 5) and a Sweet Chestnut (page 8) growing together?

The plum tree

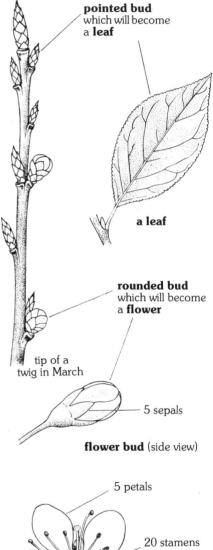

Branches	– Small tree about 3 to 4 m (10 to 12 ft) tall. – Young twigs somewhat hairy. – **Two kinds of buds** on the bare twigs. – **pointed buds** which will turn into leaves. – **rounded buds** which will turn into flowers.
Leaves	– Deciduous, alternate (see page 3), simple and slightly serrated.
Flowers	– Appear in March, **at the same time as the leaves.** They are white with short stems, arranged in groups of three. – They are **symmetrical**, and made up of 5 sepals, 5 petals, 20 or so stamens, and one pistil at the base of the cup. They are rich in nectar, and frequented by bees.
Fruits	– Ripen from July to September, according to the variety. – They are **juicy fruits,** containing a stone, inside which is the **seed**. – Their colour, shape and size varies according to type. All plums are covered with a fine grey dust, or "bloom", which rubs off easily.
Cultivation	– A hardy tree, which grows well in many places. – It can be found growing wild in the hedgerow, and on the edge of woods. – It is a native of Asia.

pointed bud
which will become a **leaf**

a leaf

rounded bud
which will become a **flower**

tip of a
twig in March

5 sepals

flower bud (side view)

5 petals

20 stamens

1 pistil

the open flower (front view)

6. Look for other fruit trees.

7. How long does it take the plum tree, the almond tree and the cherry tree to produce their fruit?

a. Open flowers. Note the pistil

b. A flowering twig: look for
the pointed buds

c. Faded flowers

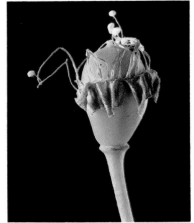

d. A young plum

e. Ripe fruit. Look at the leaves too

Cherry	Almond	Apricot
Large number of **white flowers** in groups of 2 to 8. March and April. **Fruit** ripens in June or July. Long, **serrated leaves**. Probably came from Asia.	Large **white or pink flowers,** in February or March. **Fruit** ripens in August or September. **Long, narrow leaves,** very smooth, pale green. Young twigs are also green. Native of Asia.	**White or pink flowers** from February to April. **Fruit** ripens in July. Bright green **leaves,** oval and heart-shaped at the base. Twisted branches. Native of Asia.

Apple	Pear	Peach
Pink flowers, with **yellow stamens**, growing in clusters, May or June. Pistil like that of the pear tree. **Fruit** ripens August to October. **Oval leaves**, toothed, hairy on the underside, curved veins. Native of Central and Western Asia.	**White flowers with red stamens**, in April or May. Pistil fused to the base of the flower. **Fruit** ripens July to September. **Oval leaves**, very slightly toothed, with 8 to 15 pairs of straight veins. Native of Eastern Europe and Central Asia.	Large, **bright pink flowers** in March or April. **Fruit** ripens July to October. Long, narrow **leaves**, soft and undulate. Native of China.

The lemon tree

A small **evergreen** tree, about 3 to 5 m (10 to 15 ft) tall, which is grown in warm countries such as Spain and the countries of North Africa.

The **buds** and the young leaves are red in colour and grow on **thorny twigs**. The **leaves** are slightly serrated, and have a flattened stalk which is **hinged** at the base of the blade.

The lemon tree bears fruit and flowers for most of the year. The **flowers** have a delicious smell. They have green, pointed sepals, white petals, numerous stamens and a long, pointed pistil.

The lemon is a juicy **fruit**, containing a large number of pips, which germinate easily. (Try it.) These are the **seeds**. The peel of the lemon contains oil, and the zest (the thin yellow skin) is used for flavouring cakes and pastries.

This tree is a native of India and China.

a. Flowers

b. Young leaves and flower buds

c. Young lemons

8. Draw a lemon or an apple, showing the remains of the flower.

The fig tree

The fig tree grows naturally in many areas of the world. It can be found in the Mediterranean countries, in parts of Asia, including northern India, and in Africa.

It was certainly one of the earliest fruit trees cultivated by primitive men. Then, in ancient times, figs – together with grain and olives – were considered as a basic food by all the peoples of the Mediterranean area.

The fig tree usually grows in a sunny place, against a rock or wall, often among old ruins.

It is a small tree—1 to 6 m (3 to 18 ft), with a very **twisted shape**. There are many branches, and a **smooth, grey bark**. The young twigs and leaf-stalks exude a **milky fluid** when broken, which causes skin irritation in some people. The roots often send up suckers, which themselves take root.

Two types of **buds** can be seen on the twigs in March and April.
– **Rounded buds**, which look like miniature figs. They have tiny flowers inside (a);
– **Pointed buds**, which develop into leafy shoots over several months (from April to October).

The **leaves** are large—25 cm (10 in)—and lobed. They look like broad hands (a). They are bright green, and rough on top. The underside is soft and furry.

The **fruits** ripen in September (b). The figs we eat usually come from Turkey or Africa. They can be eaten fresh, canned, or dried.

a

b

19

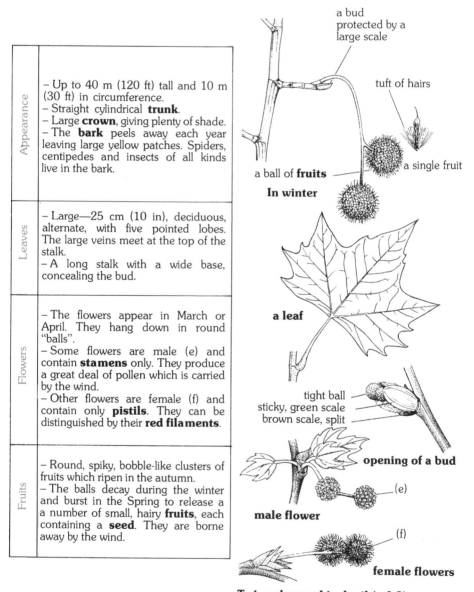

SHADY TREES
The plane

This tree is a native of the Near East and North America. It is the most common of all roadside trees, and can live for several hundred years.

Appearance	– Up to 40 m (120 ft) tall and 10 m (30 ft) in circumference. – Straight cylindrical **trunk**. – Large **crown**, giving plenty of shade. – The **bark** peels away each year leaving large yellow patches. Spiders, centipedes and insects of all kinds live in the bark.
Leaves	– Large—25 cm (10 in), deciduous, alternate, with five pointed lobes. The large veins meet at the top of the stalk. – A long stalk with a wide base, concealing the bud.
Flowers	– The flowers appear in March or April. They hang down in round "balls". – Some flowers are male (e) and contain **stamens** only. They produce a great deal of pollen which is carried by the wind. – Other flowers are female (f) and contain only **pistils**. They can be distinguished by their **red filaments**.
Fruits	– Round, spiky, bobble-like clusters of fruits which ripen in the autumn. – The balls decay during the winter and burst in the Spring to release a a number of small, hairy **fruits**, each containing a **seed**. They are borne away by the wind.

a bud protected by a large scale

tuft of hairs

a single fruit

a ball of **fruits**

In winter

a leaf

tight ball
sticky, green scale
brown scale, split

opening of a bud

(e)

male flower

(f)

female flowers

Twigs observed in April (x 0.3)

Facing page: a. Male flowers   b. Female flowers   c. Bud   d. Leaves and young fruits   e. Bark   f. Ripe fruits

21

The lime

The lime is planted everywhere as a park or avenue tree because of its beautiful foliage. It is a long-lived tree, living for up to 1,000 years. The details below refer to the large-leafed variety.

Appearance	– Up to 30 m (100 ft) tall. – Oval **crown** consisting of many many branches. – Grey **bark**, becoming fissured in old trees. – Smooth, reddish-brown **twigs**, with red, oval buds.
Leaves	– From 6 to 12 cm (2½ to 5 in) long, deciduous, alternate (see page 3), toothed, heart-shaped at the base and pointed at the tip. They are soft and hairy underneath.
Flowers	– Appear at the end of June: yellow, scented, growing in small clusters on a long, narrow wing. – Each flower consists of 5 sepals, 5 petals, and numerous stamens surrounding the pistil.
Fruits/Seeds	– Ripen in October – Hard, dry, rounded, five-sided. – Each contains one seed. – Carried by the wind. The seeds germinate at a distance from the tree.
Uses	– Flowers used to make herbal tea. – Wood used in carpentry.

serrated leaf

small scales

young velvety twig

remains of the bud scales

last year's wood

a twig in May

scar of last year's bud

a twig in winter

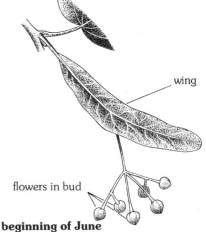

wing

flowers in bud

beginning of June

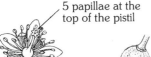

5 papillae at the top of the pistil

flower at the end of June (x 1.5) **fruit in October (x 1.5)**

9. Compare the wing of the lime, the seeds of the pine (page 13), and the hairs of the plane fruit (page 21). What do you notice?

a. A flowering branch

b. Buds and young leaves

c. Dried fruits

d. Flowers magnified 3 times

e. Flowers and young fruits on the wing

The Horse Chestnut

The Horse Chestnut was brought to Europe from the Balkans in the seventeenth century as an ornamental tree. It may reach a height of 30 m (80 to 100 ft). The **bark** is smooth in young trees, but tends to become scaly with age. The **branches** are heavy and bear large, sticky, red-brown **buds**. Each bud has a horseshoe-shaped scar beneath it.

a

The **leaves** are opposite and consist of 5 to 7 toothed leaflets, which meet at the top of the stem. They are deciduous (see page 3).

The beautiful **flower "candles"** (b) appear in May. Each flower has 5 sepals, 4 frilly petals, which are white with splashes of red and yellow, 7 long stamens, and one pistil with a rounded base and pointed tip. (The pistil is missing in some flowers.) The pollen is carried by insects, and the fertilized pistils develop into large spiny balls. These are the **fruits** of the Horse Chestnut.

b

They ripen in October. They split (c), and reveal one or two shiny, brown **seeds** – the "chestnuts". These chestnuts germinate easily (try it!) **Beware**: They are not edible.

c

10. Can the flowers without pistils produce seeds? What do you think?
11. Compare the Horse Chestnut with the Sweet Chestnut (page 8).

The acacia or robinia (False Acacia)

This is a very beautiful ornamental tree, about 15 to 25 m (50 to 80 ft) tall. It is a native of North America and has a broad, open crown with irregular branches. The **bark** is deeply fissured.

There are many suckers thrown up at the base of the trunk. It also grows wild. Its wood is used to make fence posts. The **twigs** are thorny near the buds.

The **leaves** (a) are alternate and composed of 11 to 19 soft, oval leaflets which fall individually in the autumn before the main leaf-stalk breaks away.

In June it bears clusters of beautiful **white flowers** (b), which sway in the breeze. They have a lovely smell which attracts the bees. Each corolla looks rather like a pea-flower, with 5 petals enclosing 10 stamens and one long pistil.

The **fruit** is a dry, flat, brown pod (c). It ripens in the autumn, but remains on the tree after the leaves have fallen. The **seeds** are shiny and look like small beans. They do not fall until the end of the winter. They germinate easily.

a

b

c

DECORATIVE TREES
The Judas Tree

This tree is a native of the eastern Mediterranean. It brightens our parks and gardens with its lovely colours.

The **crown** is irregular in shape. The trunk is somewhat twisted with black **bark**. The young twigs are reddish in colour.

The **leaves** are dull-green, alternate, deciduous, and have a pretty, rounded shape. They curve inwards where the stalk joins the blade. The leaves turn gold in the autumn.

At the end of April or the beginning of May, the little Judas Tree—only about 10 m (30 ft) tall—is covered with **purplish-pink flowers** which come out before the leaves. They hang in small clusters on the twigs, on the branches, and **even on the trunk!** It is a very beautiful sight.

The flowers have an unusual shape (1, 2). The calyx is large and bulbous, and the corolla consists of 5 petals enclosing 10 stamens and one long pistil. It is quite easy to see the pistil developing into a fruit.

The **fruits** are flat pods. They are red at first, but soon become brown and dry. They ripen in July or August, but stay on the tree for a long time. You can still see them in the following Spring. But the **seeds** inside have been scattered by then.

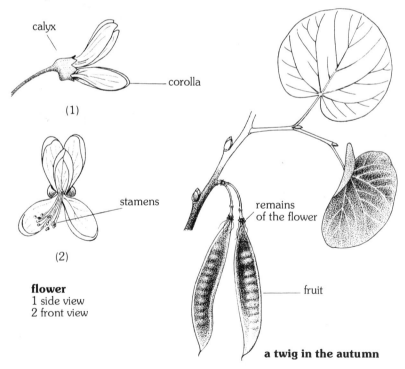

calyx

corolla

(1)

stamens

remains of the flower

(2)

flower
1 side view
2 front view

fruit

a twig in the autumn

12. Find out about other trees which have come from other countries.

a. Flowering branches

b. Flowers

c. Leaves

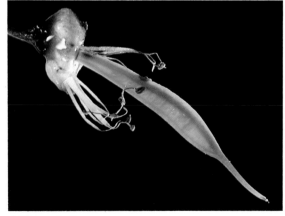
d. Young fruit

e. Dried fruits

The magnolia

This is a tall, evergreen tree —25 to 30 m (80 to 100 ft), with very beautiful flowers. It is a native of North America (a).

The large, tough, shiny **leaves** are arranged alternately.

The **flowers** appear in July and August. They look like big white globes on the end of the twigs. Each one consists of 6 to 15 petals enclosing a very large number of stamens and pistils, on top of a sort of cone (b). This cone remains on the tree once the petals have fallen, and from it develops a tight bunch of small dried **fruits** (c). Each of these fruits opens in the autumn to reveal two bright-red, hanging **seeds** (d).

a

b

c

d

The cypress

The cypress has a tall, very characteristic shape. There are many varieties. In towns the cypress is sometimes used as hedging.

The twigs are cylindrical and grow at right angles to the branch. They are covered with scaly leaves in groups of four (a).

The flowers, which are not very obvious, appear in the Spring (a). They will develop into fruits, or cones, with very hard scales (b). They contain a large number of small, light seeds, which germinate very easily. Try it: you will have a small cypress tree one month after planting the seed. The cones form in a very similar way to those of the pine (see page 12).

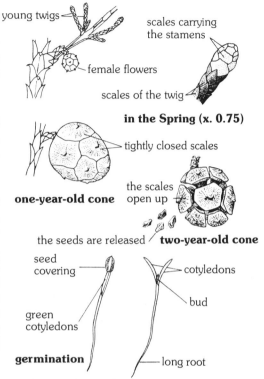

young twigs

scales carrying the stamens

female flowers

scales of the twig

in the Spring (x. 0.75)

tightly closed scales

one-year-old cone

the scales open up

the seeds are released

two-year-old cone

seed covering

cotyledons

bud

green cotyledons

germination

long root

a. Note the male flower above, and the female flower below.

b

Answers to questions

1. page 5   The oak

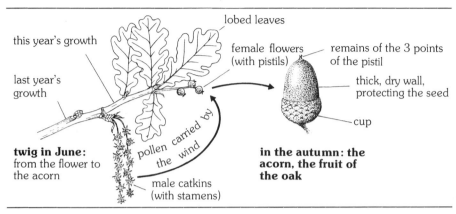

lobed leaves

this year's growth

last year's growth

female flowers (with pistils)

remains of the 3 points of the pistil

thick, dry wall, protecting the seed

cup

twig in June: from the flower to the acorn

pollen carried by the wind

male catkins (with stamens)

in the autumn: the acorn, the fruit of the oak

2. page 6   The walnut

If you break the shell gently in two, you will see inside the two thick, fatty parts of the nut, which contain the "germ". We eat the seed of the walnut tree.

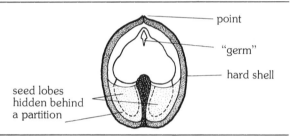

point

"germ"

hard shell

seed lobes hidden behind a partition

3. page 8   The Sweet Chestnut and the Horse Chestnut

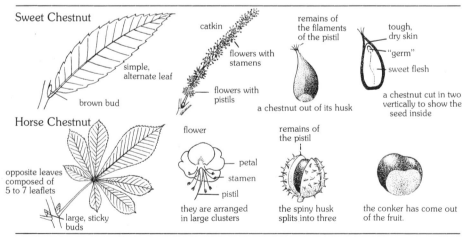

Sweet Chestnut

catkin

remains of the filaments of the pistil

tough, dry skin

flowers with stamens

simple, alternate leaf

"germ"

sweet flesh

flowers with pistils

brown bud

a chestnut out of its husk

a chestnut cut in two vertically to show the seed inside

Horse Chestnut

flower

remains of the pistil

opposite leaves composed of 5 to 7 leaflets

petal

stamen

pistil

large, sticky buds

they are arranged in large clusters

the spiny husk splits into three

the conker has come out of the fruit.

4. page 10   The willow and the oak

In the **oak**, the pollen is carried by **the wind** from the male catkins to the female flowers, which grow on the same tree.

In the **willow**, the pollen is carried by **insects** from the male flowers, which are on one tree, to the female flowers, which are on another.

5. Page 13   The Scots Pine, the oak and the Sweet Chestnut

The Scots Pine grows in all types of soil. So it can grow in the company of either the oak or the Sweet Chestnut.
The Sweet Chestnut does not like chalky soil. The oak actually prefers it! So you will never see these three trees together.

6. page 14   Fruit trees

These are trees which produce **edible fruits and seeds**: for example apricot, cherry, peach, pear, apple, plum, lemon, fig (fruits); almond, chestnut, walnut (seeds).

7. page 14   The time needed to form plums, cherries and almonds

It takes 6 to 7 months for the almond tree to produce almonds.
It takes 3 to 4 months for the cherry tree to produce cherries.
It takes 4 to 6 months for the plum tree to produce plums.

The tree which flowers first is not the quickest to produce fruit!

8. page 18   a lemon   an apple

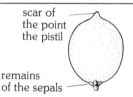

scar of
the point
the pistil

remains
of the sepals

hollow containing
dried stamens
and sepals

9. page 22   Fruits and seeds of the lime, the pine, and the plane

The wing or hairs help the fruit to be carried by the wind. The seeds will germinate some distance away.

10. page 24   The Horse Chestnut

For chestnuts (conkers) to form, the pistils must be fertilized by the pollen. Flowers without pistils cannot turn into fruit.

11. page 24   See answer 4.

12. page 26   Some trees from other parts of the world

Southern Europe: Horse Chestnut, Judas Tree, cypress.
Asia: plum, cherry, almond, fig, apple, pear, walnut, peach, apricot, lemon.
North America: plane, acacia or robinia, magnolia.

First published in the English language 1983
Revised and reprinted 1984
© Burke Publishing Company Limited 1983
Translated and adapted from *Portraits d'arbres: Collection Bornancin*
© Editions Fernand Nathan 1981

Acknowledgements
The publishers are grateful to J. Dyke for preparing the text of this edition, and to the following for permission to reproduce copyright illustrations:
 Atlas-Photo, Bornancin, Jacana, Labat, Nature, Pitch, Tarlier, Viard. Cover: Nature.
The drawings are by Josiane and Maurice Campan

CIP data
Looking at trees. – (Wake up to the World of Science).
 1. Trees
 I. Bornancin, B. II. Merigot, M.
 III. Portraits d'arbres. *English*
 IV. Series
 582.16   QK475
 ISBN 0 222 00931 4
 ISBN 0 222 00932 2 Pbk.

Burke Publishing Company Limited
Pegasus House, 116-120 Golden Lane, London EC1Y 0TL, England.
Burke Publishing (Canada) Limited
Registered Office: 20 Queen Street West, Suite 3000, Box 30, Toronto, Canada M5H 1V5.
Burke Publishing Company Inc.
Registered Office: 333 State Street, PO Box 1740, Bridgeport, Connecticut 06601, U.S.A.
Filmset in "Monophoto" Souvenir by Green Gates Studios Ltd., Hull, England.
Printed in the Netherlands by Deltaprint Holland.